THE TAILOR OF GLOSTER

MRS TITTLE-MOUSE

SQUIRREL NUTKIN

NUTS

TOM KITTEN

PETER RABBIT

D1544537

DEDICATED TO ALL PICKLES
—ESPECIALLY TO THOSE THAT GET
UPON MY GARDEN WALL

FREDERICK WARNE

Published by the Penguin Group
Registered office: 80 Strand, London, WC2R oRL
Penguin Young Readers Group, 345 Hudson Street, New York, N.Y. 10014, USA

First published 1907 by Frederick Warne
This edition with new reproductions of Beatrix Potter's book illustrations first published 2006
This edition copyright © Frederick Warne & Co. 2006
Reissued 2016
New reproductions of Beatrix Potter's book illustrations copyright © Frederick Warne & Co. 2002
Original copyright in text and illustrations © Frederick Warne & Co., 1907

Frederick Warne & Co. is the owner of all rights, copyrights and trademarks in the
Beatrix Potter character names and illustrations.

Manufactured in China

Special Markets ISBN 978-0-723-26003-5

THE TALE OF
TOM KITTEN

BY BEATRIX POTTER

FREDERICK WARNE

ONCE upon a time there were three little
kittens, and their names were Mittens, Tom
Kitten, and Moppet.

 They had dear little fur coats of their own; and
they tumbled about the doorstep and played in
the dust.

BUT one day their mother—Mrs. Tabitha Twitchit—expected friends to tea; so she fetched the kittens indoors, to wash and dress them, before the fine company arrived.

FIRST she scrubbed their faces (this one is
Moppet).

THEN she brushed their fur (this one is Mittens).

Then she combed their tails and whiskers (this is Tom Kitten).

Tom was very naughty, and he scratched.

MRS. TABITHA dressed Moppet and
Mittens in clean pinafores and tuckers; and
then she took all sorts of elegant uncomfortable
clothes out of a chest of drawers, in order to
dress up her son Thomas.

TOM KITTEN was very fat, and he had grown; several buttons burst off. His mother sewed them on again.

WHEN the three kittens were ready, Mrs. Tabitha unwisely turned them out into the garden, to be out of the way while she made hot buttered toast.

"Now keep your frocks clean, children! You must walk on your hind legs. Keep away from the dirty ash-pit, and from Sally Henny-penny, and from the pig-stye and the Puddle-ducks."

Moppet and Mittens walked down the garden path unsteadily. Presently they trod upon their pinafores and fell on their noses.

When they stood up there were several green smears!

"LET us climb up the rockery, and sit on the
garden wall," said Moppet.

They turned their pinafores back to front, and
went up with a skip and a jump; Moppet's white
tucker fell down into the road.

TOM KITTEN was quite unable to jump
when walking upon his hind legs in trousers.
He came up the rockery by degrees, breaking
the ferns, and shedding buttons right and left.

HE was all in pieces when he reached the top
of the wall.

Moppet and Mittens tried to pull him
together; his hat fell off, and the rest of his
buttons burst.

WHILE they were in difficulties, there was a
pit pat paddle pat! and the three Puddle-Ducks
came along the hard high road, marching one
behind the other and doing the goose step—
pit pat paddle pat! pit pat waddle pat!

THEY stopped and stood in a row, and stared up at the kittens. They had very small eyes and looked surprised.

THEN the two duck-birds, Rebeccah and
Jemima Puddle-duck, picked up the hat and
tucker and put them on.

MITTENS laughed so that she fell off the wall. Moppet and Tom descended after her; the pinafores and all the rest of Tom's clothes came off on the way down.

"Come! Mr. Drake Puddle-duck," said Moppet—"Come and help us to dress him! Come and button up Tom!"

MR. DRAKE
Puddle-duck
advanced in a slow
sideways manner,
and picked up the
various articles.

But he put them on
himself! They fitted
him even worse than
Tom Kitten.
"It's a very fine
morning!" said Mr.
Drake Puddle-duck.

AND he and Jemima and Rebeccah Puddle-
duck set off up the road, keeping step—pit pat,
paddle pat! pit pat, waddle pat!

THEN Tabitha Twitchit came down the garden and found her kittens on the wall with no clothes on.

SHE pulled them off the wall, smacked them, and took them back to the house.

"MY friends will arrive in a minute, and you are not fit to be seen; I am affronted," said Mrs. Tabitha Twitchit.

She sent them upstairs; and I am sorry to say she told her friends that they were in bed with the measles; which was not true.

QUITE the contrary; they were not in bed; *not* in the least.

Somehow there were very extraordinary noises over-head, which disturbed the dignity and repose of the tea party.

AND I think that some day I shall have to make another, larger, book, to tell you more about Tom Kitten!

AS for the Puddle-ducks—they went into a pond. The clothes all came off directly, because there were no buttons.

AND Mr. Drake Puddle-duck, and Jemima and Rebeccah, have been looking for them ever since.